RECOMMENDATIONS FOR

FOSTERING ENVIRONMENTAL JUSTICE

FOR

TRIBES AND INDIGENOUS PEOPLES

January 15, 2013

A Report of Recommendations
of the
National Environmental Justice Advisory Council
A Federal Advisory Committee to the U.S. Environmental Protection Agency

ACKNOWLEDGEMENTS

The National Environmental Justice Advisory Council (NEJAC) acknowledges the efforts of the NEJAC Indigenous Peoples Work Group (Work Group) in preparing the initial draft of this report. The NEJAC also acknowledges the stakeholders and community members who participated in the Council's deliberation by providing public comments. In addition, the Work Group's efforts were supported by U.S. Environmental Protection Agency (EPA) staff, notably Ms. Dona Harris, Co-Designated Federal Officer (DFO), and Mr. Daniel Gogal, Co-DFO, of the Work Group.

DISCLAIMER

NATIONAL ENVIRONMENTAL JUSTICE ADVISORY COUNCIL
List of Members

NEJAC Executive Council
Elizabeth Yeampierre, UPROSE, Brooklyn, New York (NEJAC *Chair*)
Margaret May, Ivanhoe Neighborhood Council, Kansas City, Missouri (NEJAC Vice-Chair)
Teri Blanton, Kentuckians for the Commonwealth, Berea, Kentucky
Peter Captain, Sr., Yukon River Intertribal Watershed Council, Fairbanks, Alaska
Andrea Guajardo, Conejos County Clean Water, Inc, Antonito, Colorado
Stephanie Hall, Valero Energy, San Antonio, Texas
Monica Hedstrom, White Earth Nation, White Earth, Minnesota
Effenus Henderson, Weyerhaeuser, Federal Way, Washington
Savanala 'Savi' Horne, Land Loss Prevention Project, Durham, North Carolina
Langdon Marsh, National Policy Consensus Center, Portland, Oregon
Vernice Miller-Travis, Maryland Commission on Environmental and Sustainable Communities, Bowie, Maryland
Paul Mohai, University of Michigan School of Natural Resources and Environment, Ann Arbor, Michigan
Edith Pestana, Connecticut Department of Environmental Protection, xx, Connecticut
John Ridgway, Washington State Department of Ecology,
Nia Robinson, SisterSong, Greensboro, North Carolina
Patricia Salkin, Jacob D. Fuchsberg Law Center, Touro College, Central Islip, New York
Deidre Sanders, Pacific Gas & Electric, San Francisco, California
Fatemah Shafaei, Spellman College, Atlanta, Georgia
Nicky Sheats, Center for the Urban Environment, Thomas Edison State College, Trenton, New Jersey
Paul Shoemaker, Boston Public Health Commission, Boston, Massachusetts
Kenneth Smith, Mayor, City of Kingsland, Georgia
Horace Strand, Chester Environmental Partnership, Chester, Pennsylvania
Nicholas Targ, ABA Environmental Justice Caucus, San Francisco, California
Javier Francisco Torres, Border Environment Cooperation Commission, El Paso, Texas
Kimberly Wasserman, Little Village Environmental Justice Organization, Chicago, Illinois

Victoria Robinson, Designated Federal Officer, EPA Office of Environmental Justice

Indigenous Peoples Work Group (IPWG)
Monica Hedstrom, White Earth Nation, Mahnomen, Minnesota (Work Group co-Chair)
Wahleah Johns, Black Mesa Water Coalition, Flagstaff, Arizona (Work Group co-Chair)
Peter Captain, Yukon River Intertribal Watershed Alliance, Fairbanks, Alaska
Katsi Cook, Running Strong for American Indian Youth, Washington, D.C.
Sandy Grande, Connecticut College, New London, Connecticut
Herb Lee, Jr., Pacific American Foundation, Kailua, Hawaii
Jessica Koski, Keepers of the Water, L'Anse, Michigan
Jerry Pardilla, National Tribal Environmental Council, Albuquerque, New Mexico
Brenda Dardar Robichaux, United Houma Nation, Raceland, Louisiana
Jacqueline Shirley, Native Village of Hooper Bay, Alaska

Former Member: Jolene Catron, Wind River Alliance, Fort Washakie, Wyoming

Daniel Gogal, Designated Federal Officer, EPA Office of Environmental Justice
Dona Harris, Designated Federal Officer, EPA American Indian Environmental Office

NATIONAL ENVIRONMENTAL JUSTICE ADVISORY COUNCIL

Members:

ElizabethYeampierre,
  Chair
Margaret May,
  Vice-Chair
Teri Blanton
Peter Captain, Sr.
Andrea Guajardo
Stephanie Hall
Savanala 'Savi' Horne
Monica Hedstrom
Effenus Henderson
Langdon Marsh
Vernice Miller-Travis
Paul Mohai
Edith Pestana
John Ridgway
Nia Robinson
Patricia Salkin
Deidre Sanders
Fatemeh Shafiei
Nicky Sheats
Paul Shoemaker
Kenneth Smith
Horace Strand
Nicholas Targ
Javier Francisco Torres
Kimberly Wasserman

January 15, 2013

Lisa P. Jackson
Administrator
U.S. Environmental Protection Agency
Ariel Rios Building
1200 Pennsylvania Ave., NW
Washington, DC 20460

Dear Administrator Jackson:

The National Environmental Justice Advisory Council (NEJAC) is pleased to transmit the following recommendations to you in response to your charge of October 5, 2011. In that charge, you asked the NEJAC to provide advice and recommendations about how the Agency can most effectively address the environmental justice issues in Indian country, including in Alaska and Hawaii and those facing indigenous peoples both on and off reservations. This report contains advice and recommendations about how EPA can improve the incorporation of environmental justice into: tribal environmental capacity-building and federal implementation programs; collaboration with federally-recognized tribal governments in addressing environmental justice concerns; collaboration with tribal community-based organizations and other indigenous peoples; and coordination with other federal agencies on tribal and indigenous environmental justice issues.

Key recommendations include:

- EPA should seek input and the meaningful involvement and engagement of tribal and indigenous communities, state-recognized tribes, and other indigenous stakeholders in the Agency's decision-making processes, pertaining to policies, projects and activities that may affect them and/or their traditionally used lands, waters, air and territories.
- EPA should comply with its long-standing Indian Policy principles, which has established sufficient guidance (EPA's 1984 Indian Policy, and Executive Order 12898) for the Agency to work effectively with tribal governments regarding on-reservation environmental justice issues.
- EPA should continue to recognize and support tribal authority to set environmental standards, make environmental policy decisions, and to manage environmental programs, demonstrating respect for internal tribal governmental affairs.
- EPA should elevate the role of Regional Environmental Justice and Tribal Coordinators/ Liaisons.
- EPA should create a standing Indigenous Peoples Environmental Justice Committee (or standing Subcommittee of the NEJAC) to help advise EPA to address Environmental Justice concerns.

- EPA should meaningfully consult with tribal governments and obtain community input prior to making policy or project decisions that may affect them and/or their traditionally used lands, waters, air and territories. It is equally important that both the EPA and tribal governments seek input from their tribal members whose subsistence lifeways, lands, waters and air quality maybe impacted by decisions made by tribal entities and governments.

Once again, thank you for this opportunity to provide recommendations for enhancing environmental justice in EPA's programs, particularly the tribal program and Agency's work with indigenous stakeholders.

Sincerely,

Elizabeth C. Yeampierre
Chair

cc: NEJAC Members
Robert Perciasepe, EPA Deputy Administrator
Michelle DePass, EPA Assistant Administrator for International and Tribal Affairs (OITA)
Cynthia Giles, EPA Assistant Administrator for Enforcement and Compliance Assurance
Lisa Garcia, EPA Associate Assistant Administrator for Environmental Justice
Heather Case, Acting Director, EPA Office of Environmental Justice (OEJ)
Victoria Robinson, NEJAC DFO, EPA OEJ
Daniel Gogal, NEJAC Indigenous Peoples Work Group DFO, EPA OEJ
Dona Harris, NEJAC Indigenous Peoples Work Group DFO, OITA American Indian Environment Office

TABLE OF CONTENTS

APPENDICES

NATIONAL ENVIRONMENTAL JUSTICE ADVISORY COUNCIL

Recommendations for
Fostering Environmental Justice for Tribes and Indigenous Peoples

CHAPTER 1:
BACKGROUND AND OVERVIEW

"Advanced" knowledge, innovation, technology and wealth have accelerated the insatiable need to feed, finance and advance growth and development, consuming natural resources at a rate that exceeds Mother Earth's ability to restore. At the same time, Indigenous peoples whose communities and nations[1] pre-date the settler-state have maintained their unique relationships with the land, rivers, seas and sky. But in the 500 years since western contact, indigenous peoples have experienced dispossession and disenfranchisement, rendering them one of the most vulnerable subgroups on standard measures for quality of life and sustainability such as: poor health, obesity, unemployment, teen pregnancies, high school drop-out rates, drug abuse, incarceration, etc. Despite these pressures, between 2000 and 2010, the American Indian/Alaska Native population grew by 1.1 million, a 26.7% increase; the overall U.S. population grew by 9.7% in comparison.[2] This phenomenal surge of population recovery in American Indian/Alaska Native communities is the foundation of their political and cultural recovery in the face of persistent health disparities. Thus, in order to develop a future of environmental justice[3], we must consider and account for the past.

Indigenous peoples of the United States also have a unique relationship with the federal government. Federally-recognized tribes[4] have a government-to-government relationship with the United States and have treaty-protected rights. Such rights inform standard processes for working with federal, state and local agencies to improve the welfare and economies of the tribes, such as providing support and resources for development projects on tribal lands. The frequent challenge to this model is that community tribal members who are a part of the tribal nation often have limited, and at times no, opportunity to give input on a project or proposed action in their communities.

---

[1] For the purposes of this report, the term "indigenous peoples" is an inclusive term that encompasses Native Americans/American Indians, Alaska Natives, and Native Hawaiians. While it is important to recognize the important historical and legal distinctions among the various terminologies (e.g. "American Indian" has historically been used when referencing members of federally-recognized tribes), "indigenous" has become the policy term of choice, particularly since the ratification of the United Nations Declaration of the Rights of Indigenous Peoples (UNDRIP). UN accepted definition for "Indigenous communities, peoples and nations" is "those which, having a historical continuity with pre-invasion and pre-colonial societies that developed on their territories, consider themselves distinct from other sectors of the societies now prevailing on those territories, or parts of them. They form at present non-dominant sectors of society and are determined to preserve, develop and transmit to future generations their ancestral territories, and their ethnic identity, as the basis of their continued existence as peoples, in accordance with their own cultural patterns, social institutions and legal system. [United Nations, Department of Economic and Social Affairs, Division for Social Policy and Development, Workshop on Data Collection and Disaggregation for Indigenous Peoples, New York, January 19-21, 2004, The Concept of Indigenous Peoples, Background paper prepared by the Secretariat of the Permanent Forum on Indigenous Issues, PFII/2004/WS.1/3]

[2] CS233784 – Report: Improving HIV Surveillance Among AI/AN p.6.

[3] EPA defines environmental justice as the fair treatment and meaningful involvement of all people regardless of race, color, national origin, or income with respect to the development, implementation, and enforcement of environmental laws, regulations, and policies

[4] The United States has a unique legal and political relationship with federally recognized Indian tribes, as provided by the Constitution of the United States, treaties, court decisions and Federal statutes. The Department of the Interior's current published list of federally recognized tribes is available at https://www.federalregister.gov/articles/2012/08/10/2012-19588/indian-entities-recognized-and-eligible-to-receive-services-from-the-bureau-of-indian-affairs (Aug. 10, 2012).

A.   Purpose

The National Environmental Justice Advisory Council (NEJAC) is the formal federal advisory committee chartered, pursuant to the Federal Advisory Committee Act, to provide advice and recommendations to the Administrator of the U.S. Environmental Protection Agency (EPA) about matters related to environmental justice. The NEJAC previously provided advice and recommendations to EPA regarding government-to-government consultation and the inclusion of tribal communities in environmental decision-making processes and providing for due process:

- *Consultation and Collaboration with Indian Tribal Governments and the Public Participation of Indigenous Groups and Tribal Citizens* (November 2000)
- *Meaningful Involvement and Fair Treatment by Tribal Environmental Regulatory Programs* (November 2004)

Although these documents were effective at bringing attention to these important issues and helped the Agency initiate efforts to address environmental justice issues in Indian country, in Alaska, and for indigenous peoples, a more comprehensive environmental justice policy is needed to clarify how EPA intends to work with a broader diversity of Indigenous peoples including: federally-recognized tribal governments, tribal community-based and grassroots organizations on or off the reservations, tribal members, and indigenous communities off reservations, including state-recognized tribes, Native Hawaiians and other concerned parties,

In October 2011, the EPA, through its Office of International and Tribal Affairs (OITA) and Office of Environmental Justice (OEJ), issued a Charge to the NEJAC to provide advice and recommendations about how the Agency can most effectively address the environmental justice issues in Indian country, including in Alaska and Hawaii and those facing indigenous peoples both on and off reservations. As noted in the Charge, the EPA is seeking ways to improve the incorporation of environmental justice into: (1) tribal environmental capacity-building and federal implementation programs; (2) collaboration with federally-recognized tribal governments in addressing environmental justice concerns; (3) collaboration with tribal community-based organizations and other indigenous peoples, including those who may not necessarily be federally-recognized or on an Indian reservation, to address their environmental justice concerns; and 4) coordination with other federal agencies on tribal and indigenous environmental justice issues. These areas are important to the effective implementation of the Agency's new strategy for environmental justice, "Plan EJ 2014," and EPA Administrator Lisa Jackson's priorities on tribal and environmental justice programs.

Specifically, the Agency charged the Council to consider the following specific issues:

1. What activities and mechanisms (e.g. policy, guidance, or protocol) should EPA conduct and develop to work collaboratively with indigenous community-based/grassroots organizations, and other interested stakeholders living on or off reservations, to identify and address environmental justice and other quality of life concerns and needs?

2. In fulfilling EPA's obligation to consult with tribes and work with tribes on a government-to-government basis, what are the most effective ways EPA can work with federally-recognized tribal governments to address issues of environmental justice, on and off- reservations, including those raised by tribal community-based/indigenous grassroots organizations, and other stakeholders on Indian reservations or in Alaska?

3. What organizational, regulatory, or policy hurdles exist that impede, complicate, or discourage federally-recognized tribal governments, tribal community-based/indigenous grassroots organizations, and other stakeholders on Indian reservations from effectively working together to address environmental and public health concerns in Indian country, Alaska, and in other indigenous communities?

4. What organizational, regulatory, or policy mechanisms exist that encourage federally-recognized tribal governments, tribal community-based/indigenous grassroots organizations, and other stakeholders on Indian reservations to work collaboratively on environmental and public health concerns?

5. What are the recommended means and mechanisms for EPA to coordinate and collaborate with other federal agencies to effectively provide environmental justice for indigenous peoples throughout the United States?

B.   NEJAC Indigenous Peoples Work Group

In response to the Agency's charge, the NEJAC asked EPA to establish a NEJAC Indigenous Peoples Work Group (IPWG or Work Group) to research and identify potential recommendations. The Work Group was formed in October 2011 and is comprised of eleven members of diverse backgrounds including representatives of tribal governments, indigenous grassroots groups, environmental organizations, academia, indigenous elders and indigenous youth. A list of members is shown behind the cover page of this report. Work Group members met via conference call between October 2011 through September 2012 on a regular basis to discuss findings and develop recommendations. Additionally, the NEJAC obtained public comments from additional stakeholders, including community groups, during public meetings on October 25, 2011 and September 21, 2012. The latter was a teleconference meeting specifically focused on fostering environmental justice for tribes and indigenous peoples.

The Work Group was specifically tasked with exploring, considering, and presenting findings and recommendations to the NEJAC (for submission to EPA) about how the EPA can most effectively address environmental justice issues and concerns facing indigenous peoples. The Work Group was instructed to take a broad view, and not to limit its recommendations to areas only under EPA's current tribal and environmental justice programs, but rather, to examine how to stimulate thought and action about how EPA can most effectively work with tribes and indigenous peoples to provide pathways toward environmental justice.

CHAPTER 2:
ENVIRONMENTAL JUSTICE FOR INDIGENOUS PEOPLES

Since the colonization of indigenous homelands, indigenous peoples continue to negotiate challenges to their identities. The land, waters and air indigenous peoples breathe, are not only parts of the areas they call home but also integral to who they are, to their sense of self and community. As their environs are increasingly threatened by pollution, contamination and other impacts, Indigenous peoples face a range of "environmental justice issues," such as the utilization of sustainable practices, the protection of cultural resources, sacred sites, the environment and human health, and tribal sovereignty and governance.

Addressing the issues of environmental justice in Indian country, Alaska, Hawaii, and other areas of concern to indigenous peoples, is challenging. Questions arise regarding the relationship of environmental justice to tribal sovereignty, potential impacts to the federal trust responsibility, the responsibility of the federal government to the concerns of tribal members or others, as citizens of the United States, living on reservations, and the role of federal interagency coordination to address indigenous environmental justice issues. Environmental justice considerations in tribal decision-making processes can be complicated and are often misunderstood due, in part, to multi-jurisdictional aspects of governmental authority and land tenure in Indian country. Some perceptions are that environmental justice poses a threat to tribal sovereignty, while some perceive environmental justice as a critical element for tribal decision-makers to consider in both conservation and development decisions, especially those concerning social, cultural, and spiritual equities and other relevant issues. Ultimately, federal, tribal, state, and local governments are required to provide due process when implementing federal environmental law.

Environmental justice also entails some of the foundational issues that have affected indigenous peoples for generations, such as the legacy of colonization, imposition of governance structures, lack of financial and technical resources for tribes, the pendulum of federal policies on tribes (isolation, assimilation, termination, self-determination, etc.). It pertains to current day disagreements between tribal governments and their members over the direction of a tribes' economic development, such as disputes over an emphasis on fossil fuel energy development versus an emphasis on renewable energy development, and the overall plans for the use of the tribal lands and natural resources for economic development. However, environmental justice also pertains to opportunities for greater coordination and collaboration among the tribal and federal government agencies and the tribal community-based/grassroots organizations and tribal members/interested community members to address the environmental, human health and economic development needs of the communities.

The following examples demonstrate the current challenges and opportunities facing indigenous peoples as they strive to sustain their traditional lifeways and homelands.

Sustainability of Indigenous Homelands. For example, prior to western contact in the late 17th century, Native Hawaiians developed a holistic land and ocean management system that was the result of nearly 1,500 years of observation, exploration, and innovation. The Hawaiian Islands are the most isolated land mass on the planet, yet Hawaiians were able to thrive utilizing the finite resources of each island in ways that were sustainable for a growing population. The question is how did a once proud Native people that were masters in managing the "*ahupua'a*" (the division of land from the mountain to the sea) get to a place in society that has "lost" this knowledge and practice? All four major streams that flow from the mountain to the sea, the near-shore fisheries, and many of the residential areas have succumbed to environmental pollution and degradation. For indigenous peoples in Hawaii, and on the continent, the issue of tribal relationships to land and water continue to be a pervasive and elusive factor in their ability to build a self-determined future. Today, responsibility must be shared in finding and advancing solutions for the disconnections from land and resources that exists in indigenous communities. Understanding the need to empower indigenous voices, approaches that have the potential to identify creative and long-lasting solutions founded on indigenous principles that connect indigenous peoples to their ancestral homelands, need to be utilized.

Challenges to Subsistence Lifeways. For example, the United Houma Nation, located in southern Louisiana and recognized by the State of Louisiana, is facing the ongoing injurious effects of the 2010 BP oil spill on their homelands and the concurrent violations of international law that are being perpetrated on the Nation. The Houma people have lived for centuries as bayou communities. The salt water marshes, cypress swamps, and tidal estuaries have always been the foundation of their existence. Houma families are dependent on these resources for their livelihood and life-ways. These same resources are most at risk as a result of the BP oil spill. The damage to these estuaries and eco-systems is an ecocide (the large-scale destruction of the natural environment or over-consumption of critical non-renewable resources) that will impact many Houma generations to come. The United Houma Nation is facing continuing dispossession from their lands contaminated by the spill, and the loss of medicinal and ceremonial plants to the effects of the contamination.[5] The cumulative effects of these issues increase stress on the very fabric of Houma existence.

Preservation of Cultural/Ancestral Sites. Indigenous peoples on Turtle Island (North America) are very concerned about their ancestors. Thus there is concern about potential digging up and destruction of native funerary objects and skeletal remains. In the past, projects have unearthed gravesites because informed consent was not obtained from Tribal authorities. To address these concerns, the EPA could establish local planning work groups to protect these areas. For example the Mohegan Tribe has established a planning work group that includes city agencies, the Tribe, and numerous stakeholder groups to protect the Uncas Leap site a tribal natural resource with an important cultural legacy. The Mohegan's also recognize that the surrounding neighborhoods see this area as an industrial legacy. When these cases arise the tribe(s) needs to be consulted with to facilitate the planning with other stakeholders to ensure that the historic ancestral and cultural heritage sites are preserved though negotiations.

Human Health – Reproductive Health and Healthy Living Practices. American Indians and Alaska Natives continue to define themselves as citizens of tribal nations, a primarily political - not racial - status based on lineage and kinship. Tribal kinship systems are matriarchal in worldview and consciousness, matrifocal in cultural meaning, and matrilineal in social and physiologic power. In fact, American Indian and Alaska Native women are the first environment to which present and coming tribal generations are exposed. Exposures to adverse insults such as harmful chemicals and other endocrine disrupters during critical windows of development, such as puberty and the pre-natal period, can epigenetically reprogram normal physiological responses and give rise to disease later in life. Three out of every five American Indian/Alaska Native women aged 18 to 44 years have three or more chronic conditions or risk factors[6]. Multiple stressors contribute to this vulnerability, including lack of access to culturally appropriate health care coupled with exposures to industrial chemicals, violence, poverty and food insecurity. The cumulative impact of these inequalities are brought to bear on the embodied wealth of present and coming generations, and is experienced as environmental violence at the individual and community levels.

Tribes are concerned about the reproductive health effects of exposures to toxic chemicals in the environment including food additives, preservatives, persistent organophosphates, endocrine disruptors, etc. Pollution and toxins can travel thru air, water, land, animals, fish, plants, and seeds and ultimately ending up in the food chain of our indigenous native foods. indigenous women and children are at higher health risk from contamination if breastfeeding, yet breastfeeding is a bio-resource at the foundation of indigenous subsistence economies and traditional food ways. Human breast milk supports optimum structural and functional brain development in the newborn. The

---

[5] The Houma should be protected from these threats through Article 8, 2(b), Article 10, and Article 12, 1 of the UNDRIP respectively.

[6] Amparo et al 2011

embodied wealth of present and coming generations continues to be epigenetically re-programmed by disproportionate environmental exposures through a variety of media.[7]

The cumulative effect of these and other environmental justice issues contribute to the fact that tribal communities suffer food insecurity and hunger at twice the rate of the general population.[8] Health disparities such as obesity and diabetes are in part tied to an altered diet and lifestyle in an effort to avoid exposure to environmental contamination. While Indigenous communities are working to return to traditional subsistence practices such as breastfeeding, fishing, hunting, gardening, utilizing plant medicines for disease prevention and management, and renewing cultural practices that connect their youth to Mother Earth these always are being threatened by continued assaults on their environments. Natural resources are part of the cultural capital upon which tribal economic systems, food security and indigenous spiritual practices depends.

CHAPTER 3:
FEDERAL AND TRIBAL AUTHORITY/RESPONSIBILITY FOR ENVIRONMENTAL JUSTICE

The EPA and other federal agencies have an obligation to meaningfully "consult" with federally recognized tribes if there is any possibility that a federal action, whether on or off reservation, would or have the potential to adversely affect a tribe's land, resources, treaty, or usufructuary rights or interests.[9] It is important to understand that this right is not a privilege bestowed upon tribes by the federal government, but a right, rooted in the U.S. Constitution; intrinsic to Indian treaties; required by Indian trust doctrine; affirmed by federal common law, statutes, regulations, and policies; and embodied in international legal norms.[10]

A.   Federal/EPA Authority and Responsibility Related to Environmental Justice

EPA, when implementing a federal environmental program, is to integrate and implement environmental justice in Indian country and in Alaska, as articulated in:

1) The 1984 *EPA Policy for the Administration of Environmental Programs on Indian Reservations* (EPA Indian Policy)
2) President Clinton's Executive Order 12898, *Federal Actions To Address Environmental Justice in Minority Populations and Low-Income Populations* , issued February 11, 1994 directing federal agencies to consider environmental factors that negatively affect minority and low-income community people of color
3) President Obama's recent August 2011 "Memorandum of Understanding on Environmental Justice and Executive Order 12898" (EJ MOU), embedding environmental justice principles into the mission of EPA and other federal agencies.

Fundamentally, the EPA has a trust responsibility to work effectively with federally-recognized tribal governments to address environmental justice issues. The EPA Indian Policy is intended to protect the environmental interests of Indian tribes when carrying out responsibilities that may affect

---

[7] Woodruff, http://www.ncbi.nlm.nih.gov/pmc/articles/PMC2440710/pdf/nihms40518.pdf

[8] US Commission on Civil Rights. A Quiet Crisis. Pg. 14

[9] See Lower Brule Sioux Tribe v. Deer, 911 F. Supp. 395, 401 (D.S.D. 1995) (citing Hoopa Valley Tribe v. Christie, 812 F.2d 1097 (9th Cir. 1987) (defining "meaningful" consultation).

[10] Galanda, Gabriel S. 2011. "Recent Developments in Federal Indian Consultation."

reservation communities.[11] In so doing, the EPA recognizes the authority and sovereignty of tribal governments to set environmental standards, make environmental policy decisions, and to manage programs for reservations, consistent with Agency standards and regulations. Specifically, the policy stipulates: "Tribal Governments (are) the appropriate non-Federal parties for making decisions and carrying out program responsibilities affecting Indian reservations, their environments, and the health and welfare of the reservation populace." The policy further declares, "Just as EPA's deliberations and activities have traditionally involved the interests and/or participation of State Governments, EPA will look directly to Tribal Governments to play this lead role for matters affecting reservation environments." The EPA Indian Policy also encourages cooperation between tribal, state and local governments to resolve environmental problems of mutual concern.

Moreover, the National Environmental Policy Act (NEPA) requires federal agencies to incorporate environmental considerations in their planning and decision-making. Under NEPA, the lead federal agency must consult with potentially impacted federally-recognized tribes and seek public involvement, which may include community-based/indigenous grassroots organizations and tribal members. Tribes and stakeholders can participate in all phases of the NEPA process, and if not satisfied with the federal process and record of decision, may invoke administrative and judicial remedies.

Tribal authority over nonmembers within exterior boundaries of reservation lands has also been established by Congressional statute under the Clean Air Act Amendments (CAA) of 1990. The Tribal Authority Rule (1998) authorized the EPA to treat Indian tribes in the same manner as states, so that tribes may develop and implement CAA programs within tribal reservations or in other areas subject to tribal jurisdiction. Consequently, EPA is to interact with tribes on a "government-to-government" basis as it does with states. Beyond these stipulations, there are a number of existing EPA policies and guidance documents that offer a framework to guide and improve coordination with federally-recognized tribal governments to address issues of environmental justice.

While the EPA recognizes that problems are often shared and the principle of comity[12] between equals and neighbors often serves the best interests of both, Federal Indian law, often complicates environmental justice issues within Indian reservations. The complications are in part due to the methodology for determining which sovereign government has regulatory authority. The matrix of jurisdiction and authority on Indian reservations evolves from various sources including the U.S. Constitution, treaties, federal court decisions, Congressional laws, executive orders, and federal Indian policies. As a result, issues of authority are often contested. Though tribes may have a legal grounding for juridical intervention and redress, they still require needed protection from encroachment by states and corporate entities.[13]

---

[11] In some Treaties pertaining to traditional and ceded territories, such as in the Northwest-Pacific and Great Lakes, tribe's retained customary rights to lands and resources.[11] In addition, international human rights principles under UNDRIP, recognize indigenous rights to usual and accustomed places and subsistence rights for fishing, hunting, trapping, whaling, and gathering.

[12] In law, comity specifically refers to legal reciprocity—the principle that one jurisdiction will extend certain courtesies to other nations (or other jurisdictions within the same nation), particularly by recognizing the validity and effect of their executive, legislative, and judicial acts.

[13] For example, in 1981 the U.S. Supreme Court ruled that the Crow Tribe could exercise regulatory powers over nonmembers on fee lands if the nonmembers entered into a consensual relationship with the tribes, such as a commercial contract or lease; or the nonmembers' conduct threatened the political integrity, economic security, or health and welfare of the tribe. This Supreme Court decision became a precedent for all federally recognized tribes and can be applied on a case-by-case basis. Essentially, the Montana Test allows Indian tribes to remedy some of the jurisdictional challenges on

B.   Tribal Authority and Responsibility

Today, many tribes are building their capacity to assume greater responsibility and control over environmental program management on and off their reservations. Each tribe follows its own cultural, political, and legal imperatives; thus, there is great diversity among tribal political systems and no one prescribed environmental decision-making process. That being said, tribes must exercise fairness and provide due process of law including the allowance of appeals through administrative law procedures or judicial review. Some tribes have adopted an environmental review process comparable to the National Environmental Policy Act (e.g. the Tulalip Tribes developed a model Tribal Environmental Policy Act).

The NEJAC has also identified numerous instances where tribes have defined "due process" and "meaningful involvement" within their communities based upon traditional tribal principles. These are illustrated in tribal court decisions, constitutions, codes, and policies. Community-based/indigenous grassroots organizations and other stakeholders must ascertain the existence and details of tribal decision-making processes, and follow procedures and protocols. However, what remedies exist if a tribal nation doesn't have a good system of rules in place, separation of powers, or fair enforcement?

There are additional sources of law and policy that may provide insight to EPA as the Agency works with tribes to provide for meaningful involvement and due process in tribal environmental regulatory programs. For example, Section 1302, subsection 8, of the Indian Civil Rights Act (1968), no Indian tribe in exercising powers of self-government shall "deny to any person within its jurisdiction the equal protection of its laws or deprive any person of liberty or property without due process of law." In addition to the Indian Civil Rights Act, the Agency should look to UNDRIP, international human rights policies, federal human rights legislation, and federal environmental laws and regulations.

CHAPTER 4:
CONSULTATION AND MEANINGFUL INVOLVEMENT

President Obama's November 2009 Executive Order (EO) on Tribal Consultation established a firm commitment by the federal government to ensure each federal agency develops and implements effective tribal consultation plans for its interaction with federally recognized tribes. The EO also requires each federal agency to submit an annual report to the White House on progress made in implementing their tribal consultation plans.

A.   Consultation and Meaningful Involvement under the United Nations Declaration on the Rights of Indigenous Peoples (UNDRIP)

The United States recent endorsement of the United Nation's Declaration on the Rights of Indigenous Peoples (UNDRIP) on December 16, 2010 further affirms a profound commitment to consultation and meaningful involvement with indigenous peoples:

> *"Indigenous peoples have the right to maintain and develop their political, economic and social systems or institutions, to be secure in the enjoyment of their own means of*

---

reservations and assert their inherent authority over the activities of nonmembers on reservation fee lands if it may threaten the political integrity, economic security, or health and welfare of the tribe.

subsistence and development, and to engage freely in their traditional and other economic activities." (Article 20, 1)

"Indigenous peoples have the right to the conservation and protection of the environment and the productive capacity of their lands or territories and resources. States shall establish and implement assistance programmes for indigenous peoples for such conservation and protection, without discrimination." (Article 29, 1)

A central-tenet of the UNDRIP is the recognition of indigenous peoples right to free, prior and informed consent (FPIC) as a requirement, prerequisite, and manifestation of the exercise of the fundamental, inherent right to self-determination as defined in international law. FPIC began as a medical term to guarantee the rights of patients to informed consent before any medical treatment or drug was given to them. Now it is recognized as a political right that also is applicable in many other situations facing indigenous peoples. UNDRIP has employed this construct to conclude and implement valid treaties and agreements, to have sovereignty over and protect indigenous lands and natural resources, and to develop and participate in processes that redress violations of indigenous land and treaty rights.

Under the precepts of this policy: *Free* is the absence of coercion and outside pressure, including monetary inducements (unless they are mutually agreed to as part of a settlement process), and "divide and conquer" tactics. It includes the absence of any threats or implied retaliation if the result of the decision is to say "no". *Prior* is having sufficient time to allow for information-gathering and full discussion, including translations into traditional languages, before a project starts.[14] It must take place without time pressure or constraints. A plan or project must not begin before this process is fully completed and an agreement is reached. Informed is having all the relevant information available reflecting all views and positions. This includes the input of traditional elders, spiritual leaders, subsistence practitioners and traditional knowledge holders, with adequate time and resources to consider impartial and balanced information about potential risks and benefits. *Consent* is the demonstration of clear and compelling agreement, in keeping with the decision-making structures of the indigenous peoples in question, including traditional consensus procedures. Agreements must be reached with the full participation of authorized leaders, representatives or decision-making institutions as decided by the indigenous peoples themselves.

B. Example of an Effective Tribal Consultation Plan

In response to the November 2009 Presidential Memorandum on Tribal Consultation, the EPA Policy on Consultation and Coordination with Indian Tribes was created and released for use on May 4, 2011. The Policy establishes EPA standards for the consultation process, including defining the what, when, and how of consultation; designates specific EPA personnel responsible for serving as consultation points of contact in order to promote consistency in, and coordination of, the consultation process; and establishes a management oversight and reporting structure for accountability and transparency. The Agency has developed a good foundation for conducting effective tribal consultation. However, it is too early to tell how effective EPA will be in implementing its tribal consultation policy.

---

[14] For example, a member of the Western Mining Action Network Indigenous Caucus from Alaska stated: "Imagine if you had to deal with all these processes all in the Yup'ik language with limited Yup'ik language proficiency…some of the proposed mines in Alaska are in Limited English language proficiency areas, where most of the English is very difficult to translate on the spot and the public review doesn't include translations."

C.   Examples of Effective Meaningful Public Involvement Processes

Community Action for a Renewed Environment (CARE). In Hawaii, the use of EPA's current Community Action for a Renewed Environment (CARE) program has the potential to be a very successful model in addressing environmental concerns. There are basically three reasons for this: (1) it empowers communities, both Hawaiian and non-Hawaiian, to have a meaningful stake in both identifying problems and solutions; (2) it sets up a process in which government (federal, state and local) all have a partnership role along- side the community and provides an opportunity to build relationships and trust; (3) most importantly, it empowers communities to take a pro-active role in not only identifying problems but in implementing solutions through a greater degree of ownership in the outcome.

White House Initiative on Asian Americans and Pacific Islanders. EPA is one of the designated Federal Agencies under the White House Initiative on Asian Americans and Pacific Islanders, re-established on October 14, 2009. Led by the U.S. Department of Education, the federal interagency Initiative works to improve the quality of life and opportunities for Asian Americans and Pacific Islanders by facilitating increased access to and participation in federal programs where they remain underserved. The Initiative works collaboratively with the White House Office of Public Engagement and the designated federal agencies to increase Asian American and Pacific Islander participation in programs in education, commerce, business, health, human services, housing, environment, arts, agriculture, labor and employment, transportation, justice, veterans affairs and economic and community development. For the initiative, the term "Asian American and Pacific Islander" includes persons within the jurisdiction of the United States having ancestry of any of the original peoples of East Asia, Southeast Asia, or South Asia, or any of the aboriginal, indigenous, or native peoples of Hawaii and other Pacific Islands.

D.   Example of Ineffective Public Involvement

Coal Development and Water Resource Use in Black Mesa. Despite their deep understanding of local tribal history of the Navajo Nation with regard to coal energy development, particularly in Black Mesa, Arizona, tribal residents have not been meaningfully involved or provided the opportunity for input on one of the biggest proposed coal development projects in the Southwest since the 1960s. When this project was initially proposed, there was not adequate translation into the traditional language of the Navajo, nor adequate analysis of the future impacts to quality of life, land, water, and cultural resources in Black Mesa.

CHAPTER 5:
ADVICE AND RECOMMENDATIONS

The critical components for improving the incorporation of environmental justice considerations into EPA's tribal programs generally fall under one or more of these cross-cutting themes:

(1) Collaboration with tribal community-based organizations and other indigenous peoples, including those who may not necessarily be federally-recognized or on an Indian reservation, to address their environmental justice concerns
(2) Collaboration with federally-recognized tribal governments in addressing environmental justice concerns
(3) Tribal environmental capacity-building and federal implementation programs

(4) Coordination with other federal agencies on tribal and indigenous environmental justice issues.

The following findings and associated recommendations are organized around these themes. The advice and recommendations may be both general and specific, and are provided in the spirit of seeking to identify effective opportunities for addressing the issues raised in each Charge question.

A. Collaborating with Indigenous Community-Based/Grassroots Organizations

Many government agencies fail to effectively engage or inform the public of projects or activities that may affect tribal members or the communities. EPA needs to consult with tribal governments and meaningfully engage the tribal members and tribal community-based organizations/grassroots groups when its actions or concerns may or shall impact tribal interests. Central to this respect and understanding is the recognition that indigenous peoples have a strong spiritual connection to their ancestral homelands and responsibility for care-taking that predates the formation of United States.

The following recommendations respond to the first Charge question, which asks what activities and mechanisms (e.g. policy, guidance, or protocol) should EPA conduct and develop to work collaboratively with indigenous community-based/grassroots organizations, and other interested stakeholders living on or off reservations, to identify and address environmental justice and other quality of life concerns and needs

1. **EPA should ensure that tribal members, indigenous grassroots organizations, state-recognized tribes and other interested indigenous stakeholders have the capacity to access and meaningfully participate in tribal, state and federal decision-making processes.** Such access should not be limited to traditional methods of public involvement but rather include other avenues through which information can be shared and dialogues opened. EPA should consider using online databases and convening spaces for information and dialogue. EPA also should conduct regular environmental justice calls and notifications for indigenous communities and the public. EPA may need to provide funding to ensure equitable access to web-based resources and training for computer use.

2. **EPA should seek input and the meaningful involvement and engagement of tribal and indigenous communities, state-recognized tribes, and other indigenous stakeholders in the Agency's decision-making processes, pertaining to policies, projects and activities that may affect them and/or their traditionally used lands, waters, air and territories.** EPA should hold meetings and gather input from indigenous/ tribal communities, state-recognized tribes and other indigenous members whose lands, subsistence life ways, and water and air quality may, or are expected to be, impacted by an EPA action or sources of pollution, including extractive industries. In addition, EPA should acquire input from inter-generational tribal members (elders, Indigenous speaking people, youth, college students and tribal members who work off the reservation) in addition to tribal government representatives when determining such decisions. It is advisable that the EPA consider how the concept of free, prior and informed consent (FPIC) can be effectively incorporated into the Agency's decision-making processes in a timely way to improve the environment and public health in Indian country and for indigenous communities.

3. **EPA should promote the use of existing resources and provide guidance, training and workshops on environmental justice to tribal leaders and staff, as well as to state and federal agency staff, including EPA regional staff. EPA should encourage the** development of educational materials within tribal/indigenous frameworks that explains why environmental

justice is so important and the rights of community tribal members to participate in decision-making processes that may affect their community.

4. **EPA should collaborate with tribal schools, tribal colleges and universities, and universities with Native American programs** to develop instructor workshops, curriculum development, and community-based research initiatives around environmental justice (i.e. build upon the EPA Eco-Ambassador Program). In addition, EPA should provide tribal environmental justice youth and internship opportunities. EPA should also support urban Indian environmental grant opportunities for research, monitoring and community outreach and education.

5. **EPA should work with large national organizations, like the National Congress of American Indians, the National Tribal Environmental Council, the United South and Eastern Tribes, and EPA tribal councils and caucuses, to promote environmental justice as a means for good governance.** This collaboration would improve the understanding and identify opportunities for the more effective implementation of environmental justice in Indian country.

6. **EPA should elevate the role of Regional Environmental Justice and Tribal Coordinators/ Liaisons.** Coordinators/liaisons should be well trained on environmental justice and tribal issues, and accessible and responsive to community members and grassroots groups in addition to customary relations with tribal government and environmental program staff. In an advocacy role, these coordinators/liaisons should respond and intervene in feasible and necessary ways on environmental justice issues raised by indigenous community-based groups and other interested stakeholders. This may include helping them to locate and understand information and regulatory processes, engage other relevant Agency staff, issue comments and recommendations, and organize and conduct site visits and workshops.

7. **EPA should recognize that indigenous peoples are more vulnerable to health impacts of pollution because of the subsistence life ways, geography, and low-income economies.** In doing so, EPA should provide funding for health studies for tribal communities, including state-recognized tribes, who are impacted by pollution and/or contamination of their land, subsistence life ways, and water and air quality. In addition, EPA should address the environmental and public health needs of tribal members of state-recognized tribes. For example, the impacts to the environment from pollution and contamination from the 2010 oil spill in Gulf of Mexico are greatly changing the lives and health of indigenous peoples, including members of state-recognized tribes.

8. **EPA should offer the opportunity for tribal non-governmental organizations to apply or co-apply with their tribal nation for federal funding.** As part of this effort, EPA should encourage, support and require community outreach, meaningful involvement, and public participation in its General Assistance Program (GAP) funding to tribal environmental programs. In addition, EPA should offer "Grants 101" classes with the understanding that many tribal grassroots organizations do not have the capacity to submit large competitive grant proposals and may need assistance in making sure their bylaws and internal processes are adequate to receive federal funding.

B.   **Need for Effective EPA Coordination and Cooperation with Tribal Government to Provide for Environmental Justice**

EPA must remain vigilant to the historical reality that federal policy recognizing tribes' separate political existence and sovereignty depends upon the cultural distinctiveness of tribes from the larger

American society. Institutions of tribal governance include extended kinship networks that "do not exist to reproduce or replicate dominant canons appearing in state and federal courts". This "Dilemma of Difference" occurs even within tribes, such as the diversity of spiritual expression and the social contexts of tribal community members.[15] Many federal agencies frequently fail to meaningfully consult or collaborate with tribal governments on projects or activities that may, or will, impact tribal interests. EPA has an obligation to enlarge its understanding of and support for tribally-developed environmental management approaches. These are essential policy elements that should guide Agency deliberations, clarifications, and eventual policy development to address tribal and indigenous environmental justice issues.

The following recommendations respond to the second Charge question, which asks, in fulfilling EPA's obligation to consult with tribes and work with tribes on a government-to-government basis, what are the most effective ways EPA can work with federally-recognized tribal governments to address issues of environmental justice, on and off- reservations, including those raised by tribal community-based/indigenous grassroots organizations, and other stakeholders on Indian reservations or in Alaska?

9. **EPA should comply with its long-standing Indian Policy principles, which has established sufficient guidance (EPA's 1984 Indian Policy, and Executive Order 12898) for the Agency to work effectively with tribal governments regarding on-reservation environmental justice issues.** The EPA must recognize that it cannot relinquish treaty responsibilities when it delegates programs to states. In addition, the EPA should extend enforcement of trust responsibility to important off-reservation traditionally used territories, lands, and waters—especially those with retained rights under treaties.

10. **EPA should continue to recognize and support tribal authority to set environmental standards, make environmental policy decisions, and to manage environmental programs, demonstrating respect for internal tribal governmental affairs.** EPA should provide technical assistance and program funding to tribal governments to strengthen environmental policy making processes, establish program capabilities, obtain delegated program authorities, and engage meaningfully with tribal members and the broader community.

11. **EPA should encourage tribal nations who have EPA programs or receive funding from EPA to get training and become well versed on the importance of environmental justice**, particularly as it pertains to the public participation and due process provisions in federal environmental law and administrative laws.

12. **EPA should create a standing Indigenous Peoples Environmental Justice Committee (or standing Subcommittee of the NEJAC) to help advise EPA to address Environmental Justice concerns.** Such a committee, comprised of indigenous stakeholders representatives (indigenous grassroots organizations , elders, youth, academics, state-recognized tribes, non-governmental organizations, business/industry), and federally recognized tribal government representatives who have done environmental justice work in their communities, would supplement the work of the National Tribal Caucus by focusing on the non-federally recognized tribal governments and other indigenous stakeholders environmental, public health and related economic concerns, as well as federally recognized tribal governments' EJ concerns.

---

[15] Ranco, EJ Cultural Dilemma

13. **EPA should meaningfully consult with tribal governments and obtain community input prior to making policy or project decisions that may affect them and/or their traditionally used lands, waters, air and territories.   It is equally important that both the EPA and tribal governments seek input from their tribal members whose subsistence lifeways, lands, waters and air quality maybe impacted by decisions made by tribal entities and governments.** As such, EPA should create a "space" where the voices of indigenous communities/villages/organizations and tribal community members can be heard in determining such decisions.

14. **EPA should respect the diversity of governance systems among tribes.** To ensure this effort, EPA should establish a jurisdictional matrix to determine regulatory authority needs on an individual tribal basis, due to the unique historical and legal experience of each tribe, such as implications of lost control on reservations due to allotment legacies via treaty in some cases and extensively under the General Allotment Act.

15. **EPA should also encourage greater cooperation and coordination among business/industry, tribal governments and indigenous communities/tribal members during the planning, development and implementation of projects or activities.** Many indigenous communities and tribal members feel they are excluded from the decision-making processes around development and environmental/public health protection that directly or indirectly affect their communities. EPA can promote the idea that engaging the public and potentially affected communities and citizens early and often in the decision-making process will result in greater environmental and public health protection.

16. **The EPA should consult with Tribal authorities when proposed activities may have an impact on a natural resource with a cultural legacy and ancestral areas.** When these circumstances arise the EPA should consult with Tribes and assist in facilitating planning workgroups with other stakeholders to ensure that historic ancestral and cultural heritage sites are preserved through negotiations. EPA should also coordinate with the appropriate federal and state agencies which have either federal or state statutory responsibilities to protect tribal cultural and sacred objects and sites.

C.   **Key Organizational, Regulatory, Process and Policy Issues to Provide Environmental Justice for Tribes and Indigenous Peoples**

EPA does not adequately consider in its rule-making that tribal communities are uniquely vulnerable to disproportionate exposures to pesticides and other toxic chemicals that harm the reproductive health of present and future generations.

These recommendations respond to the third and fourth Charge questions, which ask what organization, regulatory, or policy hurdles exist that impede, complicate, or discourage federally-recognized tribal governments, tribal community-based/indigenous grassroots organizations, and other stakeholders on Indian reservations from effectively working together to address environmental and public health concerns in Indian Country, Alaska and in other indigenous communities?

17. **EPA should recognize that all stakeholders are part of the problem. All stakeholders need to be a part of the solution and all roles are important.** Environmental degradation affecting the places we live has no regard for politically designated boundaries. We are all human beings, and culturally we are diverse. Solutions will likewise be diverse, reflecting the wisdom of each socio-cultural group and their distinct geographic areas.

18. **EPA should engage tribal community-based/indigenous advocacy organizations to ensure that environmental exposures of greatest interest and concern are studied and provide training in the role of media, data access, and publication access in this process.** EPA should host webinars and community level workshops on the role and authority of EPA in relation to tribes and indigenous peoples. These webinars and workshops would be facilitated by various EPA regulatory programs and include environmental/technical sessions that respond to particular community issues and concerns.

19. **EPA should support tribes in examining intersecting issues of environmental health and reproductive health through the human rights framework of the UNDRIP and emergent community engagement tools.** Such tools currently funded by EPA are the Macro-epigenetics online course at Fort Peck Tribal College and the Indian Country Environmental Hazard Assessment Program (ICEHAP) online at United Tribes Technical Institute.

20. **EPA should consider health factors associated with relevant tribal and indigenous populations, treaty-reserved resources and subsistence practices in developing standards based on human health.** This respects the unique geographical circumstances of indigenous populations related to health issues while also acknowledging federal health based standards for everyone.

21. **EPA should, in its rule-makings on the health consequences of exposures to toxic chemicals, avail itself of all disciplines that have studied toxic chemicals including neuroscience, immunology, endocrinology, oncology, pulmonology, toxicology and embryology.** Reductionism inherent in each discipline would mask sub-clinical, sub-cellular effects that another discipline would discover. For example, low dose exposures would not be detected by oncologists but these same exposures may exhibit endocrine disrupting effects that could be observed by endocrinologists or embryologists.

D.   Interagency Coordination on Tribal and Indigenous Environmental Justice Issues

Federal policies or processes need to be changed to include the voices of community members before any decision is determined, especially if a project will impact their environment, homelands and cultural and historic places. Many times federal agencies only coordinate decision making processes with tribal governments and/or officials and not tribal or indigenous communities/villages and tribal community members.

The following recommendations respond to the fifth Charge question, which asks, what are the recommended means and mechanisms for EPA to coordinate and collaborate with other federal agencies to effectively provide environmental justice for indigenous peoples throughout the United States?

22. **EPA should convene a meeting that educates federal agencies about what environmental justice means to indigenous peoples and the role of such agencies in upholding the principles of environmental justice.** Such a   convening should focus on the role of environmental justice and the rights of indigenous peoples in existing decision-   making policies in regards to energy development or any development that may pose risks to the health of people,   changes in the natural environment, and cultural and historic places. As part of this effort, EPA should:

   • Host a tour with federal agencies to see what these tribal communities and/ or villages are experiencing dealing with industries, contamination and pollution being in their backyard.

This tour will allow for indigenous community members time to express their concerns and their vision for their communities.

- Create a map that identifies all the environmental justice organizations and communities that are located on tribal lands, Indian reservations, and/or tribal villages to better engage potentially impacted communities.
- Meet with tribal governments, tribal nations (recognized and non-recognized), Hawaiian natives, Alaskan villages to ensure there is a common understanding of what environmental justice entails, particularly how it applies to indigenous peoples

23. **EPA should help other federal agencies and interagency work groups build the understanding and comprehension that the constituency of tribes is also made up of tribal members and/or tribal organizations that are impacted by decisions made by federal agencies.** When there are mutual interests, or competing interests, federal agencies need to work with the potentially impacted indigenous peoples and communities to work together to uphold the principles of environmental justice.

24. **EPA should expand and make more comprehensive the environmental justice component in the procedures and policies found in the National Environmental Policy Act and Environmental Assessment processes.** Specifically EPA should establish and promote, for all the federal processes, an "alternative" to the projects proposed. Many times projects that go through an EIS or EA do not have an alternative that could have the same economic benefits and be more culturally and environmentally friendly for the health of indigenous peoples and communities.

Appendices

Appendix A

Fostering Environmental Justice in
Indian Country, Alaska, and for Indigenous Peoples

CHARGE
October 5, 2011

BACKGROUND

Expanding the Conversation on Environmentalism and Working for Environmental Justice is one of Administrator Jackson's top priorities for EPA. Plan EJ 2014, named in recognition of the 20th anniversary of the issuance of Executive Order 12898, *Federal Actions to Address Environmental Justice in Minority Populations and Low-Income Populations,* is EPA's overarching strategy for carrying out the Administrator's priority. The National Environmental Justice Advisory Council (NEJAC), at its June 2011 meeting, requested that EPA establish a work group for the NEJAC to help it provide effective advice and recommendations to the Administrator on addressing tribal and indigenous environmental justice issues.

In the mid 1990s, EPA convened the NEJAC's Indigenous Peoples Subcommittee (IPS) in acknowledgment of the unique political status of federally-recognized tribes. This subcommittee developed two documents: 1) Consultation and Collaboration with Indian Tribal Governments and the Public Participation of Indigenous Groups and Tribal Citizens (November 2000), and 2) Meaningful Involvement and Fair Treatment by Tribal Environmental Regulatory Programs (November 2004). These documents provided advice and recommendations to EPA regarding government-to-government consultation and the inclusion of tribal communities in environmental decision-making processes and providing for due process. The IPS was decommissioned in 2005 along with all other standing NEJAC subcommittees.

Although these documents were effective at bringing attention to these important issues and helped the Agency initiate efforts to address environmental justice issues in Indian country, in Alaska, and for indigenous peoples, the Agency recognizes that it needs a comprehensive tribal and indigenous peoples environmental justice policy or established processes for addressing these issues. These processes or policy would clarify how EPA intends to work with federally-recognized tribal governments, tribal community-based and grassroots organizations on or off the reservations, and indigenous communities off reservations, including state-recognized tribes, Native Hawaiians and other concerned parties, to address environmental justice on Indian reservations, in Alaska and for indigenous peoples throughout the United States.

ISSUE

As the Agency moves forward with Plan EJ 2014, EPA is committed to develop effective mechanisms for implementing its environmental justice and other tribal priorities in Indian country, Alaska, and in other areas where indigenous peoples live and culturally use. EPA is seeking ways to improve the incorporation of environmental justice into its tribal environmental capacity building and implementation programs, and into its direct implementation of federal environmental programs on Indian reservations. EPA is also striving to work more effectively with tribal community-based organizations and other indigenous peoples not federally-recognized to address their environmental justice concerns, whether they are on or off Indian reservations, as well as improve the Agency's work with federally-recognized tribes when these entities seek involvement. These issues are relevant as the Agency implements Plan EJ 2014's cross-cutting issues and Administrator Jackson's priorities, particularly in how EPA:

- supports community-based action programs (best ways to integrate EJ principles into state, tribal, and grant work plans; promote state and tribal involvement in EJ discussions, etc.)

- fosters Administration-wide action on environmental justice,
- expands the conversation on environmentalism, as it works for environmental justice, and
- builds strong state and tribal partnerships in Indian country, Alaska and for indigenous peoples throughout the United States.

CHARGE

EPA requests that the NEJAC provide advice and recommendations on the following questions to assist the Agency in developing processes and/or policy for addressing tribal and indigenous peoples' environmental justice issues and concerns.

1. What activities and mechanisms (e.g. policy, guidance, or protocol) should EPA conduct and develop to work collaboratively with indigenous community-based/grassroots organizations, and other interested stakeholders living on or off reservations, to identify and address environmental justice and other quality of life concerns and needs?

2. In fulfilling EPA's obligation to consult with tribes and work with tribes on a government-to-government basis, what are the most effective ways EPA can work with federally-recognized tribal governments to address issues of environmental justice, on and off- reservations, including those raised by tribal community-based/indigenous grassroots organizations, and other stakeholders on Indian reservations or in Alaska?

3. What organizational, regulatory, or policy hurdles exist that impede, complicate, or discourage federally-recognized tribal governments, tribal community-based/indigenous grassroots organizations, and other stakeholders on Indian reservations from effectively working together to address environmental and public health concerns in Indian country, Alaska, and in other indigenous communities?

4. What organizational, regulatory, or policy mechanisms exist that encourage federally-recognized tribal governments, tribal community-based/indigenous grassroots organizations, and other stakeholders on Indian reservations to work collaboratively on environmental and public health concerns?

5. What are the recommended means and mechanisms for EPA to coordinate and collaborate with other federal agencies to effectively provide environmental justice for indigenous peoples throughout the United States?

The NEJAC will also be asked to provide input about the Agency's draft processes or policy for addressing tribal and indigenous peoples EJ concerns and the corresponding implementation plan(s) as they are developed by EPA.

Appendix B

The United Nations Declaration on the Rights of Indigenous Peoples can be found at
http://www.un.org/esa/socdev/unpfii/documents/DRIPS_en.pdf

United Nations Declaration
on the Rights of Indigenous Peoples

Resolution adopted by the General Assembly

[without reference to a Main Committee (A/61/L.67 and Add.1)]

61/295. United Nations Declaration on the Rights of Indigenous Peoples

The General Assembly,

Taking note of the recommendation of the Human Rights Council contained in its resolution 1/2 of 29 June 2006,[1] by which the Council adopted the text of the United Nations Declaration on the Rights of Indigenous Peoples,

Recalling its resolution 61/178 of 20 December 2006, by which it decided to defer consideration of and action on the Declaration to allow time for further consultations thereon, and also decided to conclude its consideration before the end of the sixty-first session of the General Assembly,

Adopts the United Nations Declaration on the Rights of Indigenous Peoples as contained in the annex to the present resolution.

107th plenary meeting
13 September 2007

Annex

United Nations Declaration on the Rights of Indigenous Peoples

The General Assembly,

Guided by the purposes and principles of the Charter of the United Nations, and good faith in the fulfilment of the obligations assumed by States in accordance with the Charter,

Affirming that indigenous peoples are equal to all other peoples, while recognizing the right of all peoples to be different, to consider themselves different, and to be respected as such,

---

[1] See *Official Records of the General Assembly, Sixty-first Session, Supplement No. 53* (A/61/53), part one, chap. II, sect. A.

Affirming also that all peoples contribute to the diversity and richness of civilizations and cultures, which constitute the common heritage of humankind,

Affirming further that all doctrines, policies and practices based on or advocating superiority of peoples or individuals on the basis of national origin or racial, religious, ethnic or cultural differences are racist, scientifically false, legally invalid, morally condemnable and socially unjust,

Reaffirming that indigenous peoples, in the exercise of their rights, should be free from discrimination of any kind,

Concerned that indigenous peoples have suffered from historic injustices as a result of, inter alia, their colonization and dispossession of their lands, territories and resources, thus preventing them from exercising, in particular, their right to development in accordance with their own needs and interests,

Recognizing the urgent need to respect and promote the inherent rights of indigenous peoples which derive from their political, economic and social structures and from their cultures, spiritual traditions, histories and philosophies, especially their rights to their lands, territories and resources,

Recognizing also the urgent need to respect and promote the rights of indigenous peoples affirmed in treaties, agreements and other constructive arrangements with States,

Welcoming the fact that indigenous peoples are organizing themselves for political, economic, social and cultural enhancement and in order to bring to an end all forms of discrimination and oppression wherever they occur,

Convinced that control by indigenous peoples over developments affecting them and their lands, territories and resources will enable them to maintain and strengthen their institutions, cultures and traditions, and to promote their development in accordance with their aspirations and needs,

Recognizing that respect for indigenous knowledge, cultures and traditional practices contributes to sustainable and equitable development and proper management of the environment,

Emphasizing the contribution of the demilitarization of the lands and territories of indigenous peoples to peace, economic and social progress and development, understanding and friendly relations among nations and peoples of the world,

Recognizing in particular the right of indigenous families and communities to retain shared responsibility for the upbringing, training, education and well-being of their children, consistent with the rights of the child,

Considering that the rights affirmed in treaties, agreements and other constructive arrangements between States and indigenous peoples are, in some situations, matters of international concern, interest, responsibility and character,

Considering also that treaties, agreements and other constructive arrangements, and the relationship they represent, are the basis for a strengthened partnership between indigenous peoples and States,

Acknowledging that the Charter of the United Nations, the International Covenant on Economic, Social and Cultural Rights[2] and the International Covenant on Civil and Political Rights,[2] as well as the Vienna Declaration and Programme of Action,[3] affirm the fundamental importance of the right to self-determination of all peoples, by virtue of which they freely determine their political status and freely pursue their economic, social and cultural development,

Bearing in mind that nothing in this Declaration may be used to deny any peoples their right to self-determination, exercised in conformity with international law,

Convinced that the recognition of the rights of indigenous peoples in this Declaration will enhance harmonious and cooperative relations between the State and indigenous peoples, based on principles of justice, democracy, respect for human rights, non-discrimination and good faith,

Encouraging States to comply with and effectively implement all their obligations as they apply to indigenous peoples under international instruments, in particular those related to human rights, in consultation and cooperation with the peoples concerned,

Emphasizing that the United Nations has an important and continuing role to play in promoting and protecting the rights of indigenous peoples,

---

[2] See resolution 2200 A (XXI), annex.

[3] A/CONF.157/24 (Part I), chap. III.

Believing that this Declaration is a further important step forward for the recognition, promotion and protection of the rights and freedoms of indigenous peoples and in the development of relevant activities of the United Nations system in this field,

Recognizing and reaffirming that indigenous individuals are entitled without discrimination to all human rights recognized in international law, and that indigenous peoples possess collective rights which are indispensable for their existence, well-being and integral development as peoples,

Recognizing that the situation of indigenous peoples varies from region to region and from country to country and that the significance of national and regional particularities and various historical and cultural backgrounds should be taken into consideration,

Solemnly proclaims the following United Nations Declaration on the Rights of Indigenous Peoples as a standard of achievement to be pursued in a spirit of partnership and mutual respect:

Article 1

Indigenous peoples have the right to the full enjoyment, as a collective or as individuals, of all human rights and fundamental freedoms as recognized in the Charter of the United Nations, the Universal Declaration of Human Rights[4] and international human rights law.

Article 2

Indigenous peoples and individuals are free and equal to all other peoples and individuals and have the right to be free from any kind of discrimination, in the exercise of their rights, in particular that based on their indigenous origin or identity.

Article 3

Indigenous peoples have the right to self-determination. By virtue of that right they freely determine their political status and freely pursue their economic, social and cultural development.

Article 4

Indigenous peoples, in exercising their right to self-determination, have the right to autonomy or self-government in matters relating to

---

[4] Resolution 217 A (III).

their internal and local affairs, as well as ways and means for financing their autonomous functions.

Article 5

Indigenous peoples have the right to maintain and strengthen their distinct political, legal, economic, social and cultural institutions, while retaining their right to participate fully, if they so choose, in the political, economic, social and cultural life of the State.

Article 6

Every indigenous individual has the right to a nationality.

Article 7

1.   Indigenous individuals have the rights to life, physical and mental integrity, liberty and security of person.

2.   Indigenous peoples have the collective right to live in freedom, peace and security as distinct peoples and shall not be subjected to any act of genocide or any other act of violence, including forcibly removing children of the group to another group.

Article 8

1.   Indigenous peoples and individuals have the right not to be subjected to forced assimilation or destruction of their culture.

2.   States shall provide effective mechanisms for prevention of, and redress for:

(*a*)   Any action which has the aim or effect of depriving them of their integrity as distinct peoples, or of their cultural values or ethnic identities;

(*b*)   Any action which has the aim or effect of dispossessing them of their lands, territories or resources;

(*c*)   Any form of forced population transfer which has the aim or effect of violating or undermining any of their rights;

(*d*)   Any form of forced assimilation or integration;

(*e*)   Any form of propaganda designed to promote or incite racial or ethnic discrimination directed against them.

Article 9

Indigenous peoples and individuals have the right to belong to an indigenous community or nation, in accordance with the traditions and customs of the community or nation concerned. No discrimination of any kind may arise from the exercise of such a right.

Article 10

Indigenous peoples shall not be forcibly removed from their lands or territories. No relocation shall take place without the free, prior and informed consent of the indigenous peoples concerned and after agreement on just and fair compensation and, where possible, with the option of return.

Article 11

1.   Indigenous peoples have the right to practise and revitalize their cultural traditions and customs. This includes the right to maintain, protect and develop the past, present and future manifestations of their cultures, such as archaeological and historical sites, artefacts, designs, ceremonies, technologies and visual and performing arts and literature.

2.   States shall provide redress through effective mechanisms, which may include restitution, developed in conjunction with indigenous peoples, with respect to their cultural, intellectual, religious and spiritual property taken without their free, prior and informed consent or in violation of their laws, traditions and customs.

Article 12

1.   Indigenous peoples have the right to manifest, practise, develop and teach their spiritual and religious traditions, customs and ceremonies; the right to maintain, protect, and have access in privacy to their religious and cultural sites; the right to the use and control of their ceremonial objects; and the right to the repatriation of their human remains.

2.   States shall seek to enable the access and/or repatriation of ceremonial objects and human remains in their possession through fair, transparent and effective mechanisms developed in conjunction with indigenous peoples concerned.

Article 13

1. Indigenous peoples have the right to revitalize, use, develop and transmit to future generations their histories, languages, oral traditions, philosophies, writing systems and literatures, and to designate and retain their own names for communities, places and persons.

2. States shall take effective measures to ensure that this right is protected and also to ensure that indigenous peoples can understand and be understood in political, legal and administrative proceedings, where necessary through the provision of interpretation or by other appropriate means.

Article 14

1. Indigenous peoples have the right to establish and control their educational systems and institutions providing education in their own languages, in a manner appropriate to their cultural methods of teaching and learning.

2. Indigenous individuals, particularly children, have the right to all levels and forms of education of the State without discrimination.

3. States shall, in conjunction with indigenous peoples, take effective measures, in order for indigenous individuals, particularly children, including those living outside their communities, to have access, when possible, to an education in their own culture and provided in their own language.

Article 15

1. Indigenous peoples have the right to the dignity and diversity of their cultures, traditions, histories and aspirations which shall be appropriately reflected in education and public information.

2. States shall take effective measures, in consultation and cooperation with the indigenous peoples concerned, to combat prejudice and eliminate discrimination and to promote tolerance, understanding and good relations among indigenous peoples and all other segments of society.

Article 16

1. Indigenous peoples have the right to establish their own media in their own languages and to have access to all forms of non-indigenous media without discrimination.

2. States shall take effective measures to ensure that State-owned media duly reflect indigenous cultural diversity. States, without prejudice to ensuring full freedom of expression, should encourage privately owned media to adequately reflect indigenous cultural diversity.

Article 17

1. Indigenous individuals and peoples have the right to enjoy fully all rights established under applicable international and domestic labour law.

2. States shall in consultation and cooperation with indigenous peoples take specific measures to protect indigenous children from economic exploitation and from performing any work that is likely to be hazardous or to interfere with the child's education, or to be harmful to the child's health or physical, mental, spiritual, moral or social development, taking into account their special vulnerability and the importance of education for their empowerment.

3. Indigenous individuals have the right not to be subjected to any discriminatory conditions of labour and, inter alia, employment or salary.

Article 18

Indigenous peoples have the right to participate in decision-making in matters which would affect their rights, through representatives chosen by themselves in accordance with their own procedures, as well as to maintain and develop their own indigenous decision-making institutions.

Article 19

States shall consult and cooperate in good faith with the indigenous peoples concerned through their own representative institutions in order to obtain their free, prior and informed consent before adopting and implementing legislative or administrative measures that may affect them.

Article 20

1. Indigenous peoples have the right to maintain and develop their political, economic and social systems or institutions, to be secure in the enjoyment of their own means of subsistence and development, and to engage freely in all their traditional and other economic activities.

2. Indigenous peoples deprived of their means of subsistence and development are entitled to just and fair redress.

Article 21

1. Indigenous peoples have the right, without discrimination, to the improvement of their economic and social conditions, including, inter alia, in the areas of education, employment, vocational training and retraining, housing, sanitation, health and social security.

2. States shall take effective measures and, where appropriate, special measures to ensure continuing improvement of their economic and social conditions. Particular attention shall be paid to the rights and special needs of indigenous elders, women, youth, children and persons with disabilities.

Article 22

1. Particular attention shall be paid to the rights and special needs of indigenous elders, women, youth, children and persons with disabilities in the implementation of this Declaration.

2. States shall take measures, in conjunction with indigenous peoples, to ensure that indigenous women and children enjoy the full protection and guarantees against all forms of violence and discrimination.

Article 23

Indigenous peoples have the right to determine and develop priorities and strategies for exercising their right to development. In particular, indigenous peoples have the right to be actively involved in developing and determining health, housing and other economic and social programmes affecting them and, as far as possible, to administer such programmes through their own institutions.

Article 24

1. Indigenous peoples have the right to their traditional medicines and to maintain their health practices, including the conservation of their vital medicinal plants, animals and minerals. Indigenous individuals also have the right to access, without any discrimination, to all social and health services.

2. Indigenous individuals have an equal right to the enjoyment of the highest attainable standard of physical and mental health. States shall take the necessary steps with a view to achieving progressively the full realization of this right.

Article 25

Indigenous peoples have the right to maintain and strengthen their distinctive spiritual relationship with their traditionally owned or otherwise occupied and used lands, territories, waters and coastal seas and other resources and to uphold their responsibilities to future generations in this regard.

Article 26

1.   Indigenous peoples have the right to the lands, territories and resources which they have traditionally owned, occupied or otherwise used or acquired.

2.   Indigenous peoples have the right to own, use, develop and control the lands, territories and resources that they possess by reason of traditional ownership or other traditional occupation or use, as well as those which they have otherwise acquired.

3.   States shall give legal recognition and protection to these lands, territories and resources. Such recognition shall be conducted with due respect to the customs, traditions and land tenure systems of the indigenous peoples concerned.

Article 27

States shall establish and implement, in conjunction with indigenous peoples concerned, a fair, independent, impartial, open and transparent process, giving due recognition to indigenous peoples' laws, traditions, customs and land tenure systems, to recognize and adjudicate the rights of indigenous peoples pertaining to their lands, territories and resources, including those which were traditionally owned or otherwise occupied or used. Indigenous peoples shall have the right to participate in this process.

Article 28

1.   Indigenous peoples have the right to redress, by means that can include restitution or, when this is not possible, just, fair and equitable compensation, for the lands, territories and resources which they have traditionally owned or otherwise occupied or used, and which have been confiscated, taken, occupied, used or damaged without their free, prior and informed consent.

2.   Unless otherwise freely agreed upon by the peoples concerned, compensation shall take the form of lands, territories and resources

equal in quality, size and legal status or of monetary compensation or other appropriate redress.

Article 29

1.   Indigenous peoples have the right to the conservation and protection of the environment and the productive capacity of their lands or territories and resources. States shall establish and implement assistance programmes for indigenous peoples for such conservation and protection, without discrimination.

2.   States shall take effective measures to ensure that no storage or disposal of hazardous materials shall take place in the lands or territories of indigenous peoples without their free, prior and informed consent.

3.   States shall also take effective measures to ensure, as needed, that programmes for monitoring, maintaining and restoring the health of indigenous peoples, as developed and implemented by the peoples affected by such materials, are duly implemented.

Article 30

1.   Military activities shall not take place in the lands or territories of indigenous peoples, unless justified by a relevant public interest or otherwise freely agreed with or requested by the indigenous peoples concerned.

2.   States shall undertake effective consultations with the indigenous peoples concerned, through appropriate procedures and in particular through their representative institutions, prior to using their lands or territories for military activities.

Article 31

1.   Indigenous peoples have the right to maintain, control, protect and develop their cultural heritage, traditional knowledge and traditional cultural expressions, as well as the manifestations of their sciences, technologies and cultures, including human and genetic resources, seeds, medicines, knowledge of the properties of fauna and flora, oral traditions, literatures, designs, sports and traditional games and visual and performing arts. They also have the right to maintain, control, protect and develop their intellectual property over such cultural heritage, traditional knowledge, and traditional cultural expressions.

2. In conjunction with indigenous peoples, States shall take effective measures to recognize and protect the exercise of these rights.

Article 32

1. Indigenous peoples have the right to determine and develop priorities and strategies for the development or use of their lands or territories and other resources.

2. States shall consult and cooperate in good faith with the indigenous peoples concerned through their own representative institutions in order to obtain their free and informed consent prior to the approval of any project affecting their lands or territories and other resources, particularly in connection with the development, utilization or exploitation of mineral, water or other resources.

3. States shall provide effective mechanisms for just and fair redress for any such activities, and appropriate measures shall be taken to mitigate adverse environmental, economic, social, cultural or spiritual impact.

Article 33

1. Indigenous peoples have the right to determine their own identity or membership in accordance with their customs and traditions. This does not impair the right of indigenous individuals to obtain citizenship of the States in which they live.

2. Indigenous peoples have the right to determine the structures and to select the membership of their institutions in accordance with their own procedures.

Article 34

Indigenous peoples have the right to promote, develop and maintain their institutional structures and their distinctive customs, spirituality, traditions, procedures, practices and, in the cases where they exist, juridical systems or customs, in accordance with international human rights standards.

Article 35

Indigenous peoples have the right to determine the responsibilities of individuals to their communities.

Article 36

1.   Indigenous peoples, in particular those divided by international borders, have the right to maintain and develop contacts, relations and cooperation, including activities for spiritual, cultural, political, economic and social purposes, with their own members as well as other peoples across borders.

2.   States, in consultation and cooperation with indigenous peoples, shall take effective measures to facilitate the exercise and ensure the implementation of this right.

Article 37

1.   Indigenous peoples have the right to the recognition, observance and enforcement of treaties, agreements and other constructive arrangements concluded with States or their successors and to have States honour and respect such treaties, agreements and other constructive arrangements.

2.   Nothing in this Declaration may be interpreted as diminishing or eliminating the rights of indigenous peoples contained in treaties, agreements and other constructive arrangements.

Article 38

States, in consultation and cooperation with indigenous peoples, shall take the appropriate measures, including legislative measures, to achieve the ends of this Declaration.

Article 39

Indigenous peoples have the right to have access to financial and technical assistance from States and through international cooperation, for the enjoyment of the rights contained in this Declaration.

Article 40

Indigenous peoples have the right to access to and prompt decision through just and fair procedures for the resolution of conflicts and disputes with States or other parties, as well as to effective remedies for all infringements of their individual and collective rights. Such a decision shall give due consideration to the customs, traditions, rules and legal systems of the indigenous peoples concerned and international human rights.

Article 41

The organs and specialized agencies of the United Nations system and other intergovernmental organizations shall contribute to the full realization of the provisions of this Declaration through the mobilization, inter alia, of financial cooperation and technical assistance. Ways and means of ensuring participation of indigenous peoples on issues affecting them shall be established.

Article 42

The United Nations, its bodies, including the Permanent Forum on Indigenous Issues, and specialized agencies, including at the country level, and States shall promote respect for and full application of the provisions of this Declaration and follow up the effectiveness of this Declaration.

Article 43

The rights recognized herein constitute the minimum standards for the survival, dignity and well-being of the indigenous peoples of the world.

Article 44

All the rights and freedoms recognized herein are equally guaranteed to male and female indigenous individuals.

Article 45

Nothing in this Declaration may be construed as diminishing or extinguishing the rights indigenous peoples have now or may acquire in the future.

Article 46

1. Nothing in this Declaration may be interpreted as implying for any State, people, group or person any right to engage in any activity or to perform any act contrary to the Charter of the United Nations or construed as authorizing or encouraging any action which would dismember or impair, totally or in part, the territorial integrity or political unity of sovereign and independent States.

2. In the exercise of the rights enunciated in the present Declaration, human rights and fundamental freedoms of all shall be respected. The exercise of the rights set forth in this Declaration shall be subject only to such limitations as are determined by law

and in accordance with international human rights obligations. Any such limitations shall be non-discriminatory and strictly necessary solely for the purpose of securing due recognition and respect for the rights and freedoms of others and for meeting the just and most compelling requirements of a democratic society.

3. The provisions set forth in this Declaration shall be interpreted in accordance with the principles of justice, democracy, respect for human rights, equality, non-discrimination, good governance and good faith.

Appendix C

Factsheet: **Indigenous Peoples and the Right to Free, Prior and Informed Consent**

Source: International Indian Treaty Council's Human Rights and Capacity Building Training Program, July 2008, http://www.globalforestcoalition.org/wp-content/uploads/2010/12/Short-Guide-to-Indigenous-Peoples-Rights.pdf

Indigenous Peoples and the Right to Free, Prior and Informed Consent

For Indigenous Peoples, the Right of **Free, Prior and Informed Consent (FPIC)** is a requirement, prerequisite and manifestation of the exercise of the fundamental, inherent right to Self-determination as defined in international law.

Free, Prior and Informed Consent is a basic underpinning of Indigenous Peoples' ability to conclude and implement valid Treaties and Agreements, to have sovereignty over and protect our lands and natural resources, and to develop and participate in processes that redress violations of our land and Treaty rights. It is necessary for establishing acceptable terms and criteria for negotiations with States over any and all matters affecting our Peoples', lands and ways of life.

What is Free, Prior and Informed Consent?

Free is the absence of coercion and outside pressure, including monetary inducements (unless they are mutually agreed to as part of a settlement process), and "divide and conquer" tactics. It includes the absence of any threats or implied retaliation if the results of the decision is to say "no".

Prior is having sufficient time to allow for information-gathering and full discussion, including translations into traditional languages, before a project starts. It must take place without time pressure or constraints. A plan or project must not begin before this process is fully completed and an agreement is reached.

Informed is having all the relevant information available reflecting all views and positions. This includes the input of traditional elders, spiritual leaders, subsistence practitioners and traditional knowledge holders, with adequate time and resources to consider impartial and balanced information about potential risks and benefits.

Consent is the demonstration of clear and compelling agreement, in keeping with the decision-making structures of the Indigenous Peoples in question, including traditional consensus procedures. Agreements must be reached with the full participation of authorized leaders, representatives or decision-making institutions as decided by the Indigenous Peoples themselves.

ANY process or activity which does not meet these criteria for obtaining their FPIC as put forth by the affected Indigenous peoples is subject to immediate cease and desist.

Many Indigenous Peoples, in keeping with our original instructions, are also taught to apply what could be called the principle of Free, Prior and Informed Consent. We ask for permission from the animals, plants, minerals, rocks, waters and spirits before we use places, harvest foods or medicines, dig in the earth, hunt or fish for food or ceremonial purposes. We can also understand the principle of FPIC in terms of the obligation to ask for permission before taking an action that might affect the lives or well being of others.

Photo: Ben Powless, July 2008

FPIC for Indigenous Peoples is affirmed in many International Laws and Standards

General Recommendation XXIII of the United Nations (UN) Committee on the Elimination of Racial Discrimination, the UN General Assembly's Plan of Action for the 2nd International Decade of the World's Indigenous Peoples, International Labor Organization Convention 169 and many other international instruments recognize FPIC as a right of Indigenous Peoples and obligate states (countries) to uphold this right.

The **United Nations Declaration on the Rights of Indigenous People**s explicitly affirms the Right to Free, Prior and Informed Consent and States' obligations to obtain it in many of its provisions, including:

<u>**Article 10**</u> affirms that Indigenous Peoples shall not be forcibly removed or relocated from their lands or territories without their Free, Prior and Informed Consent,

<u>**Articles 19**</u> affirms that states must obtain the Free Prior and Informed Consent of Indigenous Peoples before adopting and implementing legislative or administrative measures which may affect them;

<u>**Article 29**</u> affirms that Indigenous Peoples must give their FPIC before hazardous materials are stored or disposed of on their lands

<u>**Article 32**</u> affirms that states must obtain FPIC prior to the approval of any development project affecting Indigenous Peoples' lands and resources, *"particularly in connection with the development, utilization or exploitation of mineral, water or other resources".*

Indigenous Peoples have the inherent and inalienable right to freely determine what is best for them and for their future generations, in accordance with their own cultures and world views. Learn about and assert your human rights! Help your Nations and Peoples to become well informed about the choices they are facing, the true risks and benefits, and what is at stake.

For more information about International Indian Treaty Council's Human Rights and Capacity Building Training Program, contact: Andrea Carmen, Executive Director, at 907-745-4482 or

www.ingramcontent.com/pod-product-compliance
Lightning Source LLC
Chambersburg PA
CBHW080911290526
45795CB00007BA/2501